If you were a worm, these would look like giant blades, reaching high into the sky.

1

If no one cuts these blades of grass, they will grow high.
Little flowers will appear. But at the park, someone mows the grass,
and it becomes a bright green lawn instead.

These teeth are sharp and strong, but they aren't made to bite you—unless you're a nut!

With their sharp teeth, gray squirrels crack open acorns and other nuts. They also eat seeds and fruit.

Squirrels must chew on hard things to keep their front teeth from growing too long.

It's not a marble! It's the eye of a bird that everybody knows.

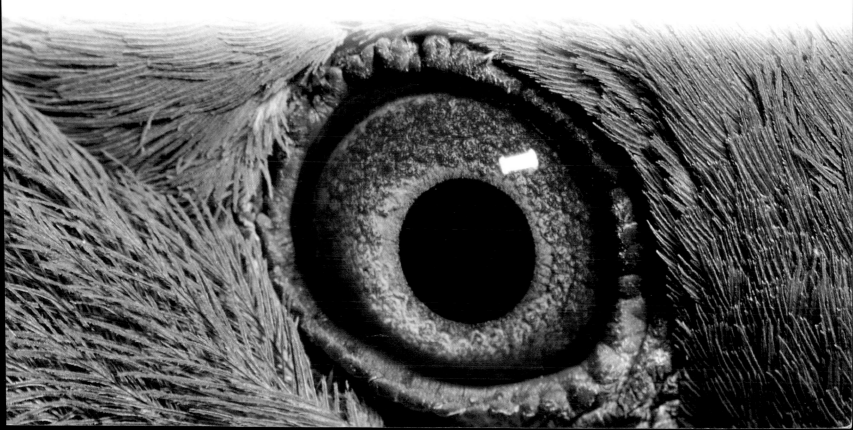

Pigeons love
parks and park
benches, too.
Some pigeons
can fly thousands
of miles to find
their way home.
But this pigeon will
probably stay in the
park for most of its life.

6

This bushy tail belongs to a masked rascal who loves to explore.

Raccoons are curious and clever.
Their paws have five long fingers,
just like your hands.
With their fingers,
raccoons find yummy
things to eat. Too bad
they don't clean up
the mess!

If you think these are hooks, you're right. Walk by them
and they'll hook onto you!

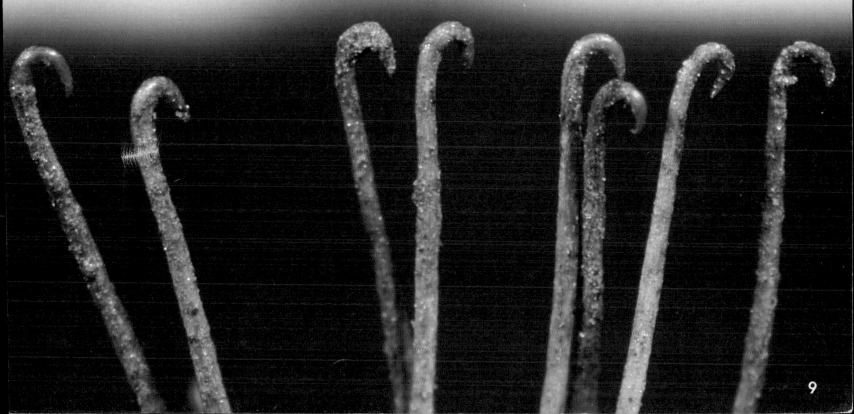

These burdock seeds have lots of little hooks that grab your clothing when you walk by. When an animal comes along, the seeds stick to its fur. This is how some seeds are carried to a new place.

This is the bill of an "ugly duckling" that grew up to be an elegant . . .

. . . swan. With its long neck, a graceful swan reaches down to find its food. It grasps underwater plants in its wide, flat bill. Then, it pulls them up from the bottom of the pond.

This nail is from a furry foot.
Some people think
it is a lucky foot.

With her front feet,
a cottontail rabbit mother
digs a nest. She scoops up
dirt and carves a "bowl"
in the ground. She lines it
with grass, leaves, and
soft fur from her coat.

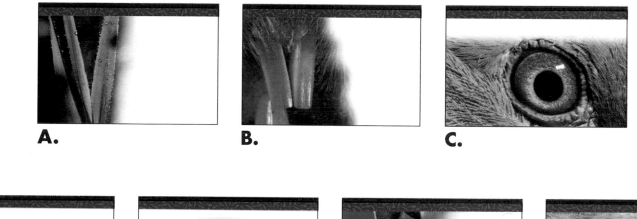

A.

B.

C.

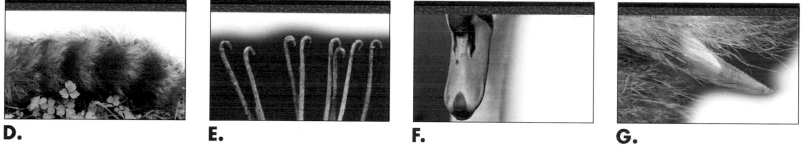

D.

E.

F.

G.

Look closely. Can you name these plants and animals?

A. Grass

B. Gray squirrel

C. Pigeon

D. Raccoon

E. Burdock

F. Swan

G. Cottontail rabbit